HOW TO MAKE MONEY ONLINE

By

Dr Chris Egbu

Author

Of

- 20 Easy Steps to Be More Productive,

- Entrepreneurial Finance-How To Raise Capital to Start Your Business

&

- Newways of Employee Empowerment

Also available on Amazon

How to Make Money Online

How to Make Money Online

Table of Contents:

Introduction

Please note that the content provided in this book is for informational purposes only. While the strategies and techniques outlined can be effective, success in making money online depends on various factors, including personal effort, market conditions, and individual circumstances.

Chapter 1: Understanding the Online Money-Making Landscape

1.1 The Advantages of Making Money Online

1.2 Common Misconceptions and Pitfalls

1.3 Assessing Your Skills and Interests

Chapter 1: Understanding the Online Money-Making Landscape

We are going to delve into the fascinating world of making money online. In this book, we will explore the advantages of online entrepreneurship, debunk common misconceptions, and guide you through assessing your skills and interests to find the perfect fit for your online money-making journey.

1.1 The Advantages of Making Money Online

Let's begin with the advantages of making money online. One of the most enticing aspects is the flexibility it offers. Imagine having the freedom to work from anywhere, at any time. Online entrepreneurship allows you to break free from the traditional 9-to-5 job and create your own schedule. This flexibility is especially beneficial for individuals who value work-life balance or have other commitments.

Another advantage is the relatively low startup costs compared to traditional businesses. Setting up an online business requires minimal investment, as you can leverage existing platforms and tools. You don't need a physical store or inventory, and marketing can be done at a fraction of the cost through social media and digital advertising.

The internet has transformed the world into a global marketplace, and online entrepreneurship allows you to tap into this vast customer base. With a well-executed online strategy, you can reach customers from all corners of the globe, expanding your business beyond geographical limitations.

Scalability is yet another advantage. Online businesses can grow rapidly if they offer valuable products or services. With the right strategies in place, you can scale your business without the constraints often associated with brick-and-mortar establishments.

1.2 Common Misconceptions and Pitfalls

Now, let's address some common misconceptions and pitfalls. It's important to be aware of these to avoid falling into traps that can hinder your online money-making journey. One misconception is the belief in overnight success and get-rich-quick schemes. While there are stories of rapid success, they are often exceptions. Building a sustainable online business takes time, effort, and dedication.

Another misconception is the idea of minimal effort and passive income. While it's true that online businesses can generate passive income streams, they require significant upfront work and ongoing maintenance. It's essential to understand that success in the online world comes from consistent effort and continuous improvement.

Now, let's discuss the pitfalls you may encounter. Information overload and analysis paralysis are common challenges. The internet is filled with an abundance of information, which can be overwhelming. It's crucial to filter through the noise and focus on actionable knowledge that will propel your online business forward.

Competition and market saturation are also concerns. Many online niches are saturated with competitors, making it challenging to stand out. However, with a unique value proposition and effective marketing strategies, you can carve out your own space in the market.

Lastly, the risk of scams and fraudulent schemes cannot be ignored. It's essential to exercise caution and do thorough research before investing time or money in any online opportunity. Stick to reputable platforms and seek advice from trusted sources.

1.3 Assessing Your Skills and Interests

Now, let's move on to assessing your skills and interests. Self-awareness is key to finding the right online money-making path. Take the time to evaluate your skills, knowledge, and experience. Identify your areas of expertise and pinpoint your strengths and weaknesses. This self-assessment will help you align your online ventures with your capabilities.

Additionally, consider your passions, hobbies, and interests. Building an online business around something you genuinely enjoy will not only make the journey more fulfilling but also increase your chances of success. When you have a genuine interest in what you do, it reflects in your work and attracts like-minded individuals.

As you assess your skills and interests, explore different online money-making avenues. There are numerous possibilities, such as e-commerce, affiliate marketing, content creation, freelancing, online education, and digital investing. Each avenue requires specific skills and offers different opportunities for growth.

To conclude, understanding the online money-making landscape is crucial for success in the digital realm. We discussed the advantages of making money online, debunked common misconceptions, and explored the importance of assessing your skills and interests.

Remember, online entrepreneurship is not a one-size-fits-all approach. It requires self-reflection, adaptability, and continuous learning. By aligning your skills and interests with the right online business model, you can embark on a rewarding journey towards financial independence and fulfillment.

Chapter 2: Setting the Foundation for Success

2.1 Goal Setting and Mindset

2.2 Building a Strong Work Ethic

2.3 Creating a Productive Workspace

Chapter 2: Setting the Foundation for Success

We are going to dive into Chapter 2 of our journey to making money online, which focuses on setting the foundation for success. In this chapter, we will explore the importance of goal setting and mindset, building a strong work ethic, and creating a productive workspace. These elements are fundamental to your online money-making journey, so let's get started!

2.1 Goal Setting and Mindset

To achieve success in any endeavor, including making money online, it is essential to set clear goals and cultivate the right mindset. Goal setting provides direction and motivation, while mindset shapes your attitude and approach towards challenges.

When setting goals, it's important to make them specific, measurable, attainable, relevant, and time-bound—also known as SMART goals. For example, instead of setting a vague goal like "make money online," you can set a SMART goal like "earn $5,000 per month through affiliate marketing within six months." This goal is specific, measurable, attainable, relevant to your online money-making journey, and has a time frame.

Once you have set your goals, it's crucial to cultivate a growth mindset. A growth mindset is characterized by the belief that abilities and intelligence can be developed through dedication and hard work. Embrace challenges, view failures as learning opportunities, and persevere in the face of setbacks. Remember that success in making money online is a journey, and setbacks are part of the process. With a growth mindset, you will approach challenges with resilience and a willingness to learn and improve.

2.2 Building a Strong Work Ethic

A strong work ethic is a critical component of success in any pursuit, including making money online. Building a strong work ethic requires discipline, consistency, and a commitment to continuous improvement.

First and foremost, establish a routine and stick to it. Set specific working hours and create a schedule that allows for focused work time. Treat your online money-making journey as a real business, dedicating the necessary time and effort to achieve your goals.

Consistency is key. Consistently engage in activities that contribute to your online business growth. Whether it's creating content, marketing, networking, or improving your skills, make it a habit to work consistently towards your goals.

Additionally, prioritize self-discipline. It's easy to get distracted in the online world, with social media, entertainment, and other tempting distractions at your fingertips. Practice self-discipline by setting boundaries, minimizing distractions, and staying focused on tasks that directly contribute to your online business.

Lastly, embrace continuous learning and improvement. The online landscape is ever-evolving, and staying up-to-date with industry trends and best practices is crucial. Invest time in expanding your knowledge, acquiring new skills, and seeking out resources and educational opportunities that can enhance your online money-making journey.

2.3 Creating a Productive Workspace

A productive workspace is vital for maintaining focus, efficiency, and creativity in your online endeavors. Here are some tips for creating a productive workspace:

First, designate a specific area for your work. This could be a separate room, a corner in your home, or a dedicated workspace in a co-working space. Having a designated area helps create a mental separation between work and personal life.

Ensure that your workspace is organized and clutter-free. A clean and organized environment promotes clarity of thought and reduces distractions. Keep essential tools and resources within reach, such as your computer, notebooks, and any other materials you frequently use.

Consider the ergonomics of your workspace. Invest in a comfortable chair and set up your desk at an appropriate height to promote good posture and prevent physical discomfort. Take breaks and incorporate movement throughout your workday to avoid prolonged sitting.

Personalize your workspace in a way that inspires and motivates you. Surround yourself with items that reflect your goals, values, and aspirations. This could include motivational quotes, vision boards, or pictures of people who inspire you.

Lastly, create a technology setup that supports your work. Ensure that you have a reliable internet connection, necessary software and tools, and a backup system for your files. A well-functioning technology setup minimizes disruptions and allows you to work efficiently.

In conclusion, setting the foundation for success is crucial in your online money-making journey. By setting clear goals, cultivating a growth mindset, building a strong work ethic, and creating a productive workspace, you are laying the groundwork for a successful and fulfilling online business venture.

I encourage you to implement these principles and continue on your path towards making money online. Remember, success is a result of consistent effort, continuous learning, and a positive mindset.

Chapter 3: Leveraging E-Commerce Platforms

3.1 Selling Physical Products Online

3.2 Dropshipping: A Lucrative Business Model

3.3 Capitalizing on Print-on-Demand Services

Chapter 3: Leveraging E-Commerce Platforms

3.1 Selling Physical Products Online

In this chapter, we will explore the power of e-commerce platforms and how they can be leveraged to sell physical products online. The rise of online shopping has opened up immense opportunities for entrepreneurs to reach a global customer base and generate significant revenue. Let's dive into the different strategies for selling physical products online.

When it comes to selling physical products online, one of the most popular approaches is setting up an online store. This involves creating your own website or utilizing e-commerce platforms like Shopify, WooCommerce, or BigCommerce.

These platforms provide user-friendly interfaces, customizable templates, and secure payment gateways, making it easier for you to showcase and sell your products.

To succeed in selling physical products online, it's crucial to identify a profitable niche. Conduct market research to understand consumer demand, competition, and pricing trends. Find a niche that aligns with your interests, has a target audience willing to purchase your products, and has room for growth.

Once you have identified your niche, source or create high-quality products to sell. You can either manufacture your products yourself, partner with manufacturers, or source products from wholesalers or dropshipping suppliers. Ensure that your products meet quality standards and offer unique value to customers.

To drive traffic and sales to your online store, employ effective marketing strategies. Utilize search engine optimization (SEO) techniques to improve your website's visibility in search engine results. Leverage social media platforms to engage with your target audience, build brand awareness, and run targeted advertising campaigns. Incorporate email marketing to nurture customer relationships and promote new products or offers.

3.2 Dropshipping: A Lucrative Business Model

Another popular business model for selling physical products online is dropshipping. Dropshipping allows you to sell products without having to handle inventory or ship products yourself.

Here's how it works:

You partner with a dropshipping supplier who stocks and ships the products on your behalf. When a customer places an order on your online store, you forward the order details to the supplier, who then fulfills and ships the products directly to the customer. As a dropshipper, you earn a profit by selling products at a higher price than the wholesale price you pay to the supplier.

Dropshipping offers several advantages. It requires minimal upfront investment since you don't need to purchase inventory in advance. It also eliminates the need for warehousing, packaging, and shipping, allowing you to focus on marketing and customer service. Dropshipping also provides the flexibility to test and scale different products quickly.

To succeed in dropshipping, it's crucial to find reliable and reputable suppliers. Conduct thorough research, read reviews, and communicate with potential suppliers to ensure they can consistently provide high-quality products and reliable shipping services. Look for suppliers who offer competitive pricing, prompt order fulfillment, and excellent customer support.

Furthermore, focus on building a strong brand and customer experience. Differentiate yourself from competitors by offering unique products, providing exceptional customer service, and creating a seamless buying experience. Invest in creating compelling product descriptions, high-quality product images, and user-friendly website design to enhance the overall shopping experience for your customers.

3.3 Capitalizing on Print-on-Demand Services

Print-on-demand (POD) services have gained popularity as a business model for selling customized and personalized products online. POD allows you to create and sell a wide range of products, such as t-shirts, mugs, phone cases, and more, with custom designs or artwork.

With POD services, you don't need to invest in inventory or equipment. Instead, you work with a POD supplier who handles the printing, packaging, and shipping of products whenever a customer places an order. This business model enables you to offer a vast array of unique designs and cater to specific customer preferences.

To leverage POD services effectively, start by identifying popular niches or trends that resonate with your target audience. Research and create compelling designs that align with those niches. Use graphic design software or work with freelance designers to create visually appealing and marketable designs.

Partner with reputable POD providers that offer a wide range of product options, high-quality printing, and reliable shipping services. Integrate their services into your online store or utilize POD-specific platforms like Printful or Printify, which seamlessly connect with popular e-commerce platforms.

Marketing is crucial to drive traffic and sales for your POD products. Utilize social media platforms, content marketing, and influencer collaborations to showcase your designs and engage with your target audience. Encourage user-generated content and leverage social proof to build trust and credibility.

In conclusion, leveraging e-commerce platforms to sell physical products online offers immense opportunities for entrepreneurs. Whether through setting up an online store, utilizing the dropshipping model, or capitalizing on print-on-demand services, you can tap into a global customer base and generate significant revenue. By identifying profitable niches, sourcing or creating high-quality products, implementing effective marketing strategies, and prioritizing customer experience, you can thrive in the online marketplace.

Chapter 4: The Power of Affiliate Marketing

4.1 Understanding Affiliate Marketing

4.2 Choosing Profitable Niches and Products

4.3 Building an Effective Affiliate Marketing Strategy

4.4 Popular affiliate marketing websites

Chapter 4: The Power of Affiliate Marketing

4.1 Understanding Affiliate Marketing

Welcome to Chapter 4! In this chapter, we will explore the power of affiliate marketing as a lucrative way to make money online. Affiliate marketing is a performance-based marketing strategy where individuals or businesses, known as affiliates, promote products or services and earn a commission for each sale or action generated through their promotional efforts.

Affiliate marketing offers a win-win situation for all parties involved. Merchants benefit from increased exposure and sales, affiliates earn commissions for their promotional efforts, and consumers gain access to valuable products or services. With the rise of e-commerce and online shopping, affiliate marketing has become a popular and effective monetization strategy.

4.2 Choosing Profitable Niches and Products

One of the key factors for success in affiliate marketing is selecting profitable niches and products to promote.

Here are some considerations to keep in mind:

Research and identify niches that have a demand for products or services. Look for niches with an active and passionate audience, as well as products or services that solve a specific problem or fulfill a particular need.

Consider the competition within your chosen niche. While competition can be a sign of a profitable market, it's important to find a balance. Look for niches where you can differentiate yourself and offer unique value to your audience.

Evaluate the commission structure and payout terms of affiliate programs. Look for programs that offer competitive commission rates and fair terms. Consider the average order value, recurring commissions, and cookie duration, which determines how long you can earn a commission from a referral.

Choose products or services that align with your audience's interests and needs. Understanding your target audience is crucial for selecting relevant and valuable products to promote. Consider their demographics, preferences, pain points, and buying behavior.

Look for reputable affiliate programs and merchants. Research the reputation and track record of the affiliate programs you're considering. Look for programs that provide reliable tracking, timely payments, and excellent support.

4.3 Building an Effective Affiliate Marketing Strategy

To maximize your success in affiliate marketing, it's essential to develop an effective strategy.

Here are some key steps to consider:

Build a strong online presence: Establish a website, blog, or social media channels to serve as your platform for promoting affiliate products. Create high-quality content that educates, entertains, and engages your audience. Focus on providing value and building trust with your audience.

Select the right promotional channels: Consider the most effective channels to reach your target audience. This could include content marketing, social media marketing, email marketing, video marketing, or a combination of these strategies. Tailor your promotional efforts to the preferences and behavior of your audience.

Create compelling content: Develop content that promotes the affiliate products in a genuine and persuasive way. Use a mix of product reviews, tutorials, comparisons, and recommendations to highlight the benefits and value of the products. Incorporate persuasive copywriting techniques and visually appealing elements to capture your audience's attention.

Incorporate affiliate links strategically: Place affiliate links within your content where they are most relevant and likely to drive conversions. Use call-to-action buttons, banners, or textual links that seamlessly integrate into your content. Be transparent with your audience about your affiliate partnerships.

Track and analyze your results: Utilize tracking tools and analytics to monitor the performance of your affiliate marketing efforts. Measure key metrics such as click-through rates, conversion rates, earnings per click, and return on investment. Identify what is working well and optimize your strategies based on data-driven insights.

Stay informed and adapt: The affiliate marketing landscape is dynamic, so it's essential to stay updated with industry trends, new products, and changes in consumer behaviour. Continuously refine and adapt your strategies based on market conditions and the needs of your audience.

4.4 Popular affiliate marketing websites

Here is a list of five popular affiliate marketing websites that are known for their reputable programs and opportunities.

Amazon Associates: Amazon's affiliate program, Amazon Associates, is one of the largest and most popular affiliate programs worldwide. It allows you to earn commissions by promoting products available on Amazon's platform.

ShareASale: ShareASale is a well-established affiliate network that offers a wide range of affiliate programs across various industries. It provides a user-friendly interface, reliable tracking, and a vast selection of merchants to choose from.

CJ Affiliate (formerly Commission Junction): CJ Affiliate is another prominent affiliate network that connects publishers with advertisers. It offers a diverse range of affiliate programs across different niches and provides robust tracking and reporting tools.

ClickBank: ClickBank is a digital marketplace that specializes in digital products such as e-books, online courses, software, and more. It has an extensive affiliate network and offers high commission rates on many of its products.

Rakuten Advertising (formerly Rakuten Affiliate Network): Rakuten Advertising is a global affiliate marketing network that provides access to numerous affiliate programs across various industries. It offers advanced tracking and reporting capabilities to help optimize your affiliate marketing efforts.

Remember that the success of your affiliate marketing endeavours depends on various factors, including your niche, the quality of products or services you promote, your marketing strategies, and your audience. It is essential to carefully research and evaluate each affiliate program to ensure it aligns with your goals and target audience.

In conclusion, affiliate marketing is a powerful and profitable strategy for making money online. By understanding the fundamentals of affiliate marketing, choosing profitable niches and products, and implementing an effective promotional strategy, you can leverage this model to generate substantial income. Remember to focus on providing value, building trust, and nurturing relationships with your audience. With dedication, persistence, and continuous learning, you can succeed in the exciting world of affiliate marketing.

Chapter 5: Unleashing the Potential of Content Creation

5.1 Blogging: Building an Online Presence

5.2 Vlogging: Engaging Audiences through Videos

5.3 Podcasting: Captivating Listeners with Audio

Chapter 5: Unleashing the Potential of Content Creation

In this chapter, we will explore the power of content creation as a means to make money online. Content creation allows individuals to express their creativity, share knowledge, and engage with audiences in various formats. We will delve into three popular forms of content creation: blogging, vlogging, and podcasting.

5.1 Blogging: Building an Online Presence

Blogging has long been a staple in the online content creation world. It involves creating and regularly updating a blog where you share written content on specific topics of interest. Blogging offers numerous opportunities to monetize your content and build a loyal audience.

Here's how you can leverage blogging effectively:

Choose a niche: Identify a niche that aligns with your interests, expertise, and audience demand. Focus on a specific topic or industry to establish yourself as an authority and attract a targeted audience.

Create valuable content: Develop high-quality, engaging, and informative articles that resonate with your audience. Provide solutions, insights, and unique perspectives on the chosen topic. Incorporate visual elements, such as images and infographics, to enhance the overall reading experience.

Build an audience: Promote your blog through various channels, including social media, email marketing, and search engine optimization (SEO) techniques. Engage with your audience by responding to comments, encouraging discussions, and offering additional resources or downloadable content.

Monetize your blog: Explore different monetization strategies such as display advertising, sponsored content, affiliate marketing, and selling digital products or services. As your blog grows, you can also consider offering premium content or membership programs for additional revenue streams.

5.2 Vlogging: Engaging Audiences through Videos

Video content has gained significant popularity in recent years, with platforms like YouTube becoming a hub for creators and viewers alike. Vlogging, or video blogging, allows you to share your thoughts, experiences, tutorials, and entertainment through videos.

Here's how you can leverage vlogging effectively:

Choose your niche: Similar to blogging, identify a niche that aligns with your interests and has a potential audience. Consider your unique personality, skills, and expertise that you can showcase through videos.

Create compelling videos: Invest in quality equipment, such as cameras, microphones, and editing software, to produce professional-looking videos. Plan your content, script or outline your videos, and focus on delivering engaging and informative content. Experiment with different video formats, such as tutorials, vlogs, interviews, or storytelling.

Optimize for discoverability: Utilize SEO techniques for video content, including keyword research, optimized titles, descriptions, and tags. Leverage social media platforms to promote your videos, collaborate with other creators, and engage with your audience.

Monetize your vlog: As your vlog gains traction and viewership, you can monetize your content through various avenues. These include YouTube's Partner Program, brand sponsorships, affiliate marketing, merchandise sales, and even crowdfunding platforms like Patreon.

5.3 Podcasting: Captivating Listeners with Audio

Podcasting has emerged as a popular medium for content creators to share their expertise, stories, and conversations through audio. Podcasts offer a unique opportunity to connect with audiences on a more intimate level while multitasking.

Here's how you can leverage podcasting effectively:

Choose your podcast niche: Identify a niche or topic that you are passionate about and has a dedicated audience. Consider the format of your podcast, such as interviews, solo episodes, storytelling, or panel discussions.

Create compelling episodes: Invest in a good quality microphone and audio editing software to ensure clear and professional sound. Plan your episodes, script or outline your content, and engage with your audience through storytelling and engaging conversations.

Publish and promote: Host your podcast on platforms like Apple Podcasts, Spotify, Google Podcasts, and others. Promote your podcast through your website, social media, guest appearances on other podcasts, and collaborations with influencers or experts in your field.

Monetize your podcast: Explore monetization options such as sponsorships, advertising, affiliate marketing, and listener donations. You can also offer premium content or exclusive bonus episodes through membership programs or platforms like Patreon.

In conclusion, content creation is a powerful way to make money online while sharing your passions and expertise with the world. Whether through blogging, vlogging, or podcasting, you have the opportunity to build a loyal audience, monetize your content through various strategies, and establish yourself as an authority in your chosen niche. Remember to consistently create valuable content, engage with your audience, and adapt to evolving trends in the digital landscape.

Chapter 6: Monetizing Social Media

6.1 Expanding Your Reach on Social Media

6.2 Influencer Marketing: Collaborating with Brands

6.3 Sponsored Posts and Advertisements

Chapter 6: Monetizing Social Media

In this chapter, we will explore the various ways to monetize social media platforms. Social media has become a powerful tool for individuals and businesses to connect with audiences, share content, and generate income. We will delve into three popular methods of monetizing social media: expanding your reach, influencer marketing, and sponsored posts/advertisements.

6.1 Expanding Your Reach on Social Media

To effectively monetize your social media presence, it's crucial to expand your reach and grow your following.

Here are some strategies to consider:

Define your target audience: Understand your target audience's demographics, interests, and preferences. Tailor your content to resonate with your audience and provide value to them.

Consistent and quality content: Regularly post high-quality content that is engaging, informative, and visually appealing. Use a mix of text, images, videos, and other media formats to capture your audience's attention.

Utilize hashtags: Research and use relevant hashtags to increase the discoverability of your content. Hashtags help users find your posts when they search for specific topics or keywords.

Engage with your audience: Respond to comments, messages, and inquiries from your followers. Encourage discussions, ask questions, and actively participate in conversations related to your niche.

Collaborate with other creators: Partner with other social media influencers or content creators to cross-promote each other's content. This can help expand your reach to their audiences and vice versa.

Utilize analytics: Use social media analytics tools to track the performance of your posts and understand what content resonates best with your audience. Adjust your strategies based on data-driven insights.

6.2 Influencer Marketing: Collaborating with Brands

Influencer marketing has become a prevalent method for brands to reach their target audience through social media. As an influencer, you can collaborate with brands and earn income through sponsored content.

Here's how you can leverage influencer marketing:

Identify your niche and brand partnerships: Determine your niche and the brands that align with your interests and values. Research and reach out to brands that may be interested in collaborating with you.

Develop a media kit: Create a media kit that showcases your social media reach, engagement metrics, audience demographics, and previous brand collaborations. A media kit helps brands understand your influence and the value you can provide.

Negotiate partnerships: When collaborating with brands, negotiate terms such as compensation, content requirements, exclusivity, and disclosure guidelines.

Ensure that the partnership aligns with your audience's interests and maintains authenticity.

Create sponsored content: Develop sponsored content that integrates the brand's products or services seamlessly into your posts. Maintain transparency by clearly disclosing sponsored partnerships to your audience.

Track and report results: Provide brands with analytics and performance reports to showcase the impact of the sponsored content. This helps build trust and encourages future collaborations.

6.3 Sponsored Posts and Advertisements

Another way to monetize social media is through sponsored posts and advertisements. Brands may approach you to create content or share their advertisements with your audience.

Here's how you can effectively monetize through sponsored posts and advertisements:

Choose relevant brands: Partner with brands that align with your niche and have products or services that would be of interest to your audience. Maintain authenticity and avoid promoting products that don't resonate with your audience.

Create engaging sponsored content: Develop sponsored posts that are visually appealing, informative, and entertaining. Incorporate the brand's message seamlessly into your content to maintain your unique voice and style.

Utilize social media advertising features: Take advantage of social media platforms' advertising features to promote sponsored posts and advertisements directly to your audience. This can help increase reach and visibility.

Maintain transparency: Clearly disclose sponsored content and advertisements to your audience. Transparency builds trust and ensures that your audience understands the nature of the content they are consuming.

Track performance: Monitor the performance of sponsored posts and advertisements using social media analytics. Analyze engagement metrics, click-through rates, and conversions to assess the effectiveness of the campaigns.

In conclusion, social media provides numerous opportunities to monetize your online presence. By expanding your reach, engaging in influencer marketing collaborations, and creating sponsored posts and advertisements, you can generate income while leveraging your social media platforms. Remember to maintain authenticity, provide value to your audience, and choose partnerships and promotions that align with your niche and audience's interests.

Chapter 7: Exploring Online Freelancing Opportunities

7.1 Freelancing Platforms and Job Marketplaces

7.2 Freelancing in Writing and Translation

7.3 Web Development and Design

7.4 Popular Online Websites for Freelancers

Chapter 7: Exploring Online Freelancing Opportunities

In this chapter, we will delve into the world of online freelancing and the various opportunities it presents. Freelancing allows individuals to offer their skills and services to clients from around the world, providing flexibility and the potential for financial independence. We will explore freelancing platforms and job marketplaces, as well as specific freelance opportunities in writing and translation, web development, and design.

7.1 Freelancing Platforms and Job Marketplaces

Freelancing platforms and job marketplaces have revolutionized the way people find and offer freelance work. These online platforms connect freelancers with clients seeking their specific skills.

Here are some popular freelancing platforms to consider:

Upwork: Upwork is one of the largest freelancing platforms, offering a wide range of job categories. It allows freelancers to create profiles, showcase their portfolios, and bid on projects posted by clients.

Fiverr: Fiverr is a platform that focuses on micro-jobs or gigs. Freelancers create "gigs" offering specific services at predetermined prices. Clients can browse these gigs and hire freelancers directly.

Freelancer: Freelancer is a global freelancing platform with a vast array of job categories. It provides opportunities for freelancers to bid on projects or contests posted by clients.

Guru: Guru is a platform that connects freelancers with businesses seeking their expertise. It allows freelancers to create profiles, showcase their work, and apply for jobs posted by clients.

When using freelancing platforms, it's important to create a compelling profile, highlight your skills and experience, and actively seek out projects that align with your expertise.

7.2 Freelancing in Writing and Translation

Writing and translation are popular freelance opportunities that offer flexibility and the ability to work remotely.

Here's how you can leverage your skills in these areas:

Writing: Freelance writing encompasses a wide range of opportunities, including content writing, copywriting, ghostwriting, and technical writing. Develop a portfolio of your work, showcase your expertise in specific niches, and actively search for writing gigs on freelancing platforms. You can also reach out to businesses, content agencies, or publications directly to offer your services.

Translation: If you are fluent in multiple languages, freelance translation can be a lucrative opportunity. Specialize in specific language pairs and industries, such as legal, medical, or technical translation. Register on translation-specific platforms like ProZ or offer your services on general freelancing platforms. Building a strong reputation and maintaining accuracy and professionalism are essential in the translation field.

7.3 Web Development and Design

Web development and design are in high demand as businesses and individuals seek to establish and enhance their online presence.

 Here's how you can pursue freelance opportunities in these areas:

Web Development: If you have coding skills, freelance web development can be a profitable venture. Specialize in front-end or back-end development, or offer full-stack development services. Showcase your portfolio of websites or web applications you have created, and actively seek projects on freelancing platforms or through networking in relevant communities.

Design: Freelance design opportunities range from graphic design to user interface (UI) and user experience (UX) design. Develop a strong portfolio showcasing your design skills, and highlight your expertise in specific design software or industries. Freelancing platforms, social media platforms, and design communities can serve as valuable resources for finding clients.

In both web development and design, staying up to date with the latest trends, technologies, and best practices is essential. Continuous learning and honing your skills will help you remain competitive in the freelance market.

7.4 Popular Online Websites for Freelancers

Here are five popular online websites for freelancers:

Upwork: Upwork is one of the largest freelance platforms, connecting freelancers with clients in various fields such as writing, design, programming, marketing, and more. It offers a wide range of job opportunities and provides tools for freelancers to showcase their skills and build their portfolios.

Fiverr: Fiverr is a marketplace where freelancers can offer their services in a variety of categories, including graphic design, writing, digital marketing, video editing, and more. Freelancers create "gigs" with specific services and set their own prices, making it a flexible platform for freelancers of different skill levels.

Freelancer: Freelancer is an online platform that connects freelancers with clients worldwide. It offers a range of job categories such as web development, graphic design, writing, translation, and more. Freelancers can bid on projects posted by clients and compete for work opportunities.

Toptal: Toptal is a platform that focuses on connecting freelancers with top-tier clients. It specializes in high-quality freelancers in fields such as software development, design, and finance. Toptal has a rigorous screening process to ensure that freelancers meet their high standards.

Guru: Guru is a freelance marketplace that offers a wide range of job categories, including programming, design, writing, administrative support, and more. It provides tools for freelancers to showcase their work, collaborate with clients, and manage projects.

These platforms provide opportunities for freelancers to find work, connect with clients, and showcase their skills. It's important to carefully review each platform, understand their fee structures, and read reviews from other freelancers to find the best fit for your skills and goals.

In conclusion, online freelancing opens up a world of opportunities for individuals to offer their skills and services globally. Whether through freelancing platforms and job marketplaces, or by specializing in writing and translation, web development, or design, you can create a successful freelance career. Remember to build a strong online presence, showcase your expertise, and actively seek out projects that align with your skills and interests.

Chapter 8: Capitalizing on Online Education

8.1 Creating and Selling Online Courses

8.2 Tutoring and Teaching Online

8.3 Monetizing Your Knowledge and Expertise

Chapter 8: Capitalizing on Online Education

In this chapter, we will explore the vast opportunities for capitalizing on online education. The digital age has transformed the way people learn, opening up avenues for individuals to create and sell online courses, offer tutoring and teaching services, and monetize their knowledge and expertise.

We will delve into the following areas: creating and selling online courses, tutoring and teaching online, and monetizing your knowledge and expertise.

8.1 Creating and Selling Online Courses

Online courses have gained immense popularity as people seek to learn new skills and acquire knowledge conveniently from their homes. Creating and selling online courses can be a lucrative venture.

Here's how you can get started:

Identify your expertise: Determine your area of expertise and the subject matter in which you can provide value to learners. It could be anything from business and marketing to photography, language learning, or personal development.

Plan your course content: Outline the course structure and break it down into modules or lessons. Create engaging and comprehensive content, including videos, written materials, quizzes, and assignments. Ensure that the course is well-organized and delivers a clear learning outcome.

Choose a platform: Select a platform to host and sell your online course. Popular platforms include Udemy, Teachable, Coursera, and Skillshare. Research each platform's features, pricing, and audience reach to determine the best fit for your course.

Create promotional materials: Develop compelling promotional materials, including a course description, video trailer, and engaging visuals. Clearly communicate the benefits and value of your course to potential learners.

Market your course: Utilize various marketing channels to promote your course. Leverage social media platforms, email marketing, content marketing, and collaborations with influencers or relevant websites to reach your target audience. Encourage satisfied learners to leave reviews and testimonials.

Provide ongoing support: Offer support and engage with your learners throughout the course. Respond to their questions and provide clarification when needed. Encourage discussions and create a sense of community among your learners.

8.2 Tutoring and Teaching Online

Online tutoring and teaching have become increasingly popular, offering individuals the opportunity to share their knowledge and provide personalized instruction to learners.

Here's how you can capitalize on this:

Determine your subjects and target audience: Identify the subjects or areas in which you can provide tutoring or teaching services. Determine your target audience, whether it's school students, college students, professionals, or individuals seeking specific skills.

Choose a tutoring platform or create your own: Select a tutoring platform such as Tutor.com, Wyzant, or VIPKid, which connect tutors with learners. Alternatively, you can create your own tutoring website or offer services through video conferencing platforms like Zoom or Skype.

Set competitive rates: Research the market rates for tutoring or teaching services in your subject area and geographic location. Price your services competitively while considering your qualifications, experience, and the value you provide.

Advertise your services: Promote your tutoring or teaching services through online channels such as social media, education forums, and local community groups. Create a professional profile that highlights your qualifications, teaching approach, and testimonials from satisfied learners.

Provide a personalized learning experience: Tailor your teaching methods to meet the individual needs of your learners. Offer support, feedback, and guidance to help them succeed in their learning journey.

8.3 Monetizing Your Knowledge and Expertise

Beyond creating online courses and offering tutoring services, there are additional ways to monetize your knowledge and expertise.

Consider the following options:

Writing ebooks or digital guides: Share your knowledge by writing ebooks or digital guides on specific topics. Self-publishing platforms like Amazon Kindle Direct Publishing make it easy to distribute and monetize your written work.

Consulting and coaching: Offer consulting services or one-on-one coaching sessions in your area of expertise. This could involve providing strategic advice, guidance, or mentorship to individuals or businesses.

Speaking engagements and webinars: Capitalize on your expertise by offering speaking engagements or hosting webinars. You can collaborate with event organizers, and industry associations, or create your own webinars and charge a fee for participation.

Affiliate marketing: Recommend products or services relevant to your niche through affiliate marketing. Earn a commission for each sale or referral made through your unique affiliate links.

Membership sites and exclusive content: Create a membership site or offer exclusive content to your audience. Charge a subscription fee, providing premium content, resources, or access to a community of like-minded individuals.

Remember to continually enhance your knowledge and stay updated in your field of expertise. Building a strong reputation and establishing yourself as an authority will help attract learners and clients.

In conclusion, the rise of online education presents numerous opportunities to capitalize on your knowledge and expertise. By creating and selling online courses, offering tutoring and teaching services, and monetizing your knowledge through ebooks, consulting, or speaking engagements, you can generate income while making a positive impact on learners around the world.

Chapter 9: Entering the World of Digital Investing

9.1 Understanding Cryptocurrencies and Blockchain

9.2 Stock Trading and Investment Platforms

9.3 Peer-to-Peer Lending and Crowdfunding

Chapter 9: Entering the World of Digital Investing

In this chapter, we will explore the world of digital investing, which has opened up new opportunities for individuals to participate in financial markets and alternative investment platforms. We will delve into the following areas: understanding cryptocurrencies and blockchain, stock trading and investment platforms, and peer-to-peer lending and crowdfunding.

9.1 Understanding Cryptocurrencies and Blockchain

Cryptocurrencies, such as Bitcoin and Ethereum, have gained significant attention in recent years. They are digital or virtual currencies that use cryptography for secure transactions and operate on decentralized networks called blockchains.

Here's what you need to know:

Learn about blockchain technology: Blockchain is a distributed ledger technology that records transactions across multiple computers, ensuring transparency and security. Understand the basics of how blockchain works and its potential applications beyond cryptocurrencies.

Research different cryptocurrencies: There are thousands of cryptocurrencies available in the market. Research and familiarize yourself with the most prominent ones, including Bitcoin, Ethereum, Ripple, and Litecoin. Understand their features, use cases, and market dynamics.

Stay updated with news and trends: The cryptocurrency market is highly dynamic and subject to rapid changes. Stay informed about the latest news, regulatory developments, and market trends to make informed investment decisions.

Choose a cryptocurrency exchange: To invest in cryptocurrencies, you'll need to choose a reputable cryptocurrency exchange. Popular exchanges include Coinbase, Binance, Kraken, and Gemini. Research their security measures, fees, and user experience before selecting one.

Understand the risks: Cryptocurrency investments come with risks, including price volatility, regulatory uncertainties, and security vulnerabilities. Only invest what you can afford to lose and consider diversifying your portfolio to manage risk.

How To Make Money with Cryptocurrencies and Blockchain

Making money with cryptocurrencies and blockchain can be approached in several ways.

Here are a few common methods:

Trading and Investing: Cryptocurrency trading involves buying and selling cryptocurrencies on exchanges to take advantage of price fluctuations. Traders aim to buy low and sell high within short timeframes. Investing, on the other hand, involves holding cryptocurrencies for longer periods, anticipating their value to increase over time. Both trading and investing require research, analysis, and risk management skills.

Mining: Mining involves using computational power to validate and secure transactions on blockchain networks. Miners are rewarded with newly minted cryptocurrencies for their contributions. However, mining can be resource-intensive and may require specialized hardware and technical knowledge.

Staking: Staking is a process where users hold and "stake" their cryptocurrencies in a wallet to support the operations of a proof-of-stake (PoS) blockchain network. In return, they receive rewards in the form of additional cryptocurrency tokens. Staking often requires users to lock up their funds for a specific period.

Running Masternodes: Certain cryptocurrencies, such as Dash and PIVX, offer masternode systems. Masternodes are full nodes on a blockchain network that perform additional functions, such as facilitating instant transactions or providing privacy features. Running a masternode requires holding a specific amount of cryptocurrency as collateral, and in return, node operators earn rewards.

Participating in Initial Coin Offerings (ICOs) and Token Sales: ICOs and token sales are fundraising methods used by blockchain projects to raise capital. By participating in these events, investors can purchase tokens at an early stage, hoping that their value will increase once the project launches or gains traction. However, it's essential to conduct thorough research on the project, team, and token economics before investing.

Providing Services: You can offer services related to cryptocurrencies and blockchain technology. This could include developing blockchain applications, providing consulting or advisory services, conducting audits, writing content, or creating educational resources. As the industry grows, there is an increasing demand for specialized expertise.

Remember, engaging with cryptocurrencies and blockchain involves risks, including price volatility, regulatory changes, and security vulnerabilities. It's crucial to educate yourself, stay updated on market trends, and consider your risk tolerance before getting involved. Consulting with financial and legal professionals is advisable to ensure compliance with local regulations and to make informed investment decisions.

9.2 Stock Trading and Investment Platforms

Digital platforms have made stock trading and investment accessible to individual investors.

Here's how you can enter the world of stock trading and investment:

Educate yourself about stock market basics: Familiarize yourself with fundamental concepts such as stocks, bonds, exchange-traded funds (ETFs), and mutual funds. Understand how stock markets function, how to analyze companies, and how to assess investment opportunities.

Choose a stock trading platform: Select an online brokerage platform that suits your needs. Consider factors such as fees, trading tools, research resources, and user interface. Popular platforms include Robinhood, TD Ameritrade, E*TRADE, and Interactive Brokers.

Open a brokerage account: Complete the account opening process with your chosen brokerage platform. Provide the required information and funds to start trading. Understand the account types available, such as individual or retirement accounts, and their respective tax implications.

Develop an investment strategy: Define your investment goals, risk tolerance, and time horizon. Create an investment strategy that aligns with your objectives. Consider factors such as asset allocation, diversification, and long-term versus short-term trading approaches.

Conduct research and analysis: Before making investment decisions, conduct thorough research on companies and industries. Utilize financial statements, news sources, analyst reports, and market data to assess investment opportunities.

Practice risk management: Implement risk management techniques, such as setting stop-loss orders and diversifying your portfolio. Regularly review and adjust your investments based on changing market conditions.

9.3 Peer-to-Peer Lending and Crowdfunding

Peer-to-peer (P2P) lending and crowdfunding platforms offer alternative investment opportunities outside of traditional financial markets.

Here's how you can explore these avenues:

Understand P2P lending: P2P lending platforms connect borrowers directly with lenders, bypassing traditional financial institutions. Research different P2P lending platforms and understand their loan structures, interest rates, default rates, and borrower profiles.

How Does P2P Lending Work?

Peer-to-peer (P2P) lending, also known as social lending or marketplace lending, is a form of lending that connects borrowers directly with individual lenders through online platforms, bypassing traditional financial institutions.

Here's how P2P lending generally works:

Borrower Application: Individuals or small businesses seeking loans submit loan applications to P2P lending platforms. The applications typically include information about the borrower's creditworthiness, the purpose of the loan, and the desired loan amount.

Credit Evaluation: P2P lending platforms assess the creditworthiness of borrowers using various criteria, such as credit scores, income verification, and risk assessment models. Some platforms also consider non-traditional factors, such as education or employment history.

Investor Participation: On the lender side, individual investors review available loan listings on the P2P platform and decide which loans to fund based on their risk appetite and investment goals. Investors can typically contribute small amounts to fund a portion of a loan, diversifying their investment across multiple borrowers.

Loan Funding: Once the loan is fully funded by multiple investors, the borrower receives the loan amount. In some cases, the platform may contribute a partial amount to complete the loan if it is not fully funded by investors.

Loan Repayment: Borrowers make regular repayments, typically monthly, including both principal and interest. The P2P platform collects the payments from borrowers and distributes them to the participating investors, minus any platform fees.

Examples of reliable P2P lending platforms include:

LendingClub: LendingClub is one of the largest and most well-known P2P lending platforms in the United States. It offers personal loans, business loans, and patient financing for medical procedures.

Prosper: Prosper is another established P2P lending platform that connects borrowers and investors in the United States. It offers personal loans for various purposes, such as debt consolidation, home improvement, and small business financing.

Funding Circle: Funding Circle is a P2P lending platform focused on business loans. It operates in several countries, including the United Kingdom, the United States, Germany, and the Netherlands.

Mintos: Mintos is a European P2P lending marketplace that connects investors with loan originators across various countries and loan types, including personal loans, mortgages, and business loans.

Zopa: Zopa is a UK-based P2P lending platform that primarily offers personal loans. It was one of the first P2P lending platforms to launch globally and has a strong track record.

It's important to conduct thorough research, consider the platform's reputation, borrower vetting processes, interest rates, fees, and user reviews before participating in P2P lending. Additionally, carefully assess your own risk tolerance and diversify your investments across multiple loans to mitigate risk.

Assess crowdfunding opportunities: Crowdfunding platforms allow individuals to invest in startups, real estate projects, or other ventures. Research different crowdfunding platforms and evaluate the investment opportunities available. Understand the risks and potential returns associated with each project.

Conduct due diligence: Conduct thorough due diligence before investing in P2P lending or crowdfunding projects. Assess the credibility of borrowers or project initiators, review financial projections, and evaluate the associated risks. Consider diversifying your investments across multiple projects to mitigate risk.

Stay updated with regulations: P2P lending and crowdfunding investments are subject to regulations that vary by jurisdiction. Stay informed about the legal requirements, investor protections, and any changes in regulations that may affect your investments.

Monitor your investments: Regularly monitor your P2P lending loans or crowdfunding investments. Stay updated on project developments, repayment statuses, and any potential risks. Consider building a diversified portfolio across different P2P lending platforms or crowdfunding projects.

As with any investment, it's important to conduct thorough research, understand the risks involved, and make informed decisions based on your financial goals and risk tolerance. Stay updated with the latest developments in the digital investing space to adapt your strategies accordingly.

Chapter 10: Scaling Your Online Business

10.1 Automation and Outsourcing

10.2 Building a Team

10.3 Expanding Your Revenue Streams

Chapter 10: Scaling Your Online Business

In this chapter, we will delve into strategies for scaling your online business and taking it to the next level. We will explore the following areas: automation and outsourcing, building a team, and expanding your revenue streams.

10.1 Automation and Outsourcing

To scale your online business efficiently, automation and outsourcing can be powerful tools.

Here's how you can leverage them:

Identify repetitive tasks: Take stock of the tasks that are repetitive, time-consuming, or can be easily automated. This could include aspects like customer support, data entry, social media scheduling, or email marketing.

Implement automation tools: Research and invest in automation tools that can streamline your business operations. For example, you can use customer relationship management (CRM) software to automate lead generation and management, or project management tools to streamline workflow and collaboration.

This is how to use customer relationship management (CRM) software to automate lead generation and management.

To automate lead generation and management using Customer Relationship Management (CRM) software, you can follow these steps:

Define Lead Generation Criteria: Determine the criteria that define a qualified lead for your business. This could include demographic information, buying behaviour, or engagement with your marketing campaigns.

Integrate Lead Capture: Integrate lead capture forms on your website, landing pages, or other marketing channels. CRM software often provides tools to create and embed these forms, allowing you to collect lead information directly into the CRM system.

Lead Scoring and Segmentation: Set up lead scoring rules within the CRM software to assign a value to each lead based on their characteristics and behaviour. This helps prioritize and segment leads for more targeted marketing and sales efforts.

Automated Lead Nurturing: Use the CRM software's automation features to set up email marketing campaigns and workflows that deliver personalized content and engage leads at various stages of the buyer's journey. This can include sending relevant resources, offers, or follow-up messages based on lead behaviour or specific triggers.

Sales Funnel Management: Utilize the CRM's pipeline and opportunity management features to track and manage leads as they progress through the sales funnel. This includes assigning leads to sales representatives, tracking interactions, and setting reminders for follow-ups.

Reporting and Analytics: Leverage the reporting and analytics capabilities of the CRM software to gain insights into lead generation and management. Monitor key metrics, such as lead conversion rates, sales pipeline performance, and campaign effectiveness, to optimize your strategies.

Now, here are five CRM software options that can help automate lead generation and management:

Salesforce: Salesforce is a widely used CRM platform offering comprehensive lead management features, automation capabilities, and integrations with other marketing tools.

HubSpot CRM: HubSpot CRM provides a free yet robust CRM solution with lead capture forms, lead scoring, workflow automation, and email marketing features.

Zoho CRM: Zoho CRM offers lead management, automation, and email marketing tools. It provides customizable workflows and integrates with other Zoho applications for a seamless experience.

Pipedrive: Pipedrive is a CRM designed to streamline sales processes, including lead management. It offers visual sales pipelines, automation features, and email integration.

Insightly: Insightly is a CRM platform that includes lead management, workflow automation, email marketing, and reporting capabilities, suitable for small to medium-sized businesses.

Remember to evaluate each CRM software based on your specific needs, budget, scalability, and integration requirements to choose the one that best aligns with your business goals.

Outsource non-core tasks: Identify tasks that are not directly related to your core business functions and consider outsourcing them. This could involve hiring freelancers or virtual assistants to handle activities like content creation, graphic design, administrative tasks, or accounting.

Utilize freelancing platforms: Platforms like Upwork, Freelancer, or Fiverr can connect you with talented freelancers across various fields. Take the time to vet potential freelancers, review their portfolios, and communicate your requirements clearly to ensure successful outsourcing partnerships.

Maintain clear communication: When working with freelancers or outsourcing tasks, establish clear communication channels and expectations. Provide detailed instructions, set deadlines, and maintain regular check-ins to ensure that projects are progressing smoothly.

10.2 Building a Team

As your online business grows, building a dedicated team can help you scale operations and expand your reach.

Consider the following steps:

Assess your needs: Determine the roles and skill sets required to support your growing business. This could include positions such as marketing specialists, customer support representatives, developers, or project managers.

Define job descriptions: Clearly define the roles and responsibilities for each position you plan to hire. Outline the required qualifications, experience, and any specific skills or certifications necessary.

Recruit top talent: Utilize various recruitment channels to attract qualified candidates. This could involve posting job openings on relevant job boards, leveraging professional networks, or working with recruitment agencies. Conduct thorough interviews and reference checks to ensure a good fit.

Foster a positive work culture: Create a positive work environment that promotes collaboration, innovation, and growth. Offer competitive compensation packages, provide opportunities for professional development, and establish clear communication channels within the team.

Delegate effectively: As you build your team, delegate tasks and responsibilities to empower your employees. Clearly communicate expectations and provide the necessary resources and support to ensure their success.

Embrace remote work: Consider remote work options, which can enable you to tap into a global talent pool. Leverage tools like project management software, video conferencing, and collaborative platforms to facilitate remote team collaboration.

10.3 Expanding Your Revenue Streams

Scaling your online business involves diversifying and expanding your revenue streams.

Here are some strategies to consider:

Add new products or services: Identify opportunities to develop and offer new products or services that complement your existing offerings. Conduct market research to understand customer demand and preferences in order to create offerings that resonate.

Explore new markets: Consider expanding into new markets or geographic regions. Adapt your marketing strategies to cater to the specific needs and preferences of those markets. Conduct thorough market research to understand the competitive landscape and potential customer base.

Develop strategic partnerships: Collaborate with other businesses or influencers in your industry to create strategic partnerships. This could involve joint marketing campaigns, cross-promotions, or co-branded offerings that help expand your reach and customer base.

Create passive income streams: Explore opportunities to generate passive income through avenues like affiliate marketing, digital product sales, or online courses. These income streams can provide ongoing revenue with minimal ongoing effort.

Leverage advertising and sponsorship: If appropriate for your business, consider partnering with advertisers or sponsors who align with your brand. This can provide an additional revenue stream while also increasing your visibility and credibility.

Continuously test and optimize: As you expand your revenue streams, track and analyze the performance of each initiative. Continuously test and optimize your strategies to maximize profitability and ensure a positive return on investment.

Scaling your online business requires careful planning, effective delegation, and strategic decision-making. By leveraging automation, building a talented team, and diversifying your revenue streams, you can position your business for growth and long-term success.

Chapter 11: Overcoming Challenges and Staying Motivated

11.1 Dealing with Competition and Market Changes

11.2 Managing Time and Avoiding Burnout

11.3 Embracing Continuous Learning and Adaptation

Chapter 11: Overcoming Challenges and Staying Motivated

In this chapter, we will discuss strategies for overcoming challenges and staying motivated as an entrepreneur in the digital age. We will cover the following areas: dealing with competition and market changes, managing time avoiding burnout, and embracing continuous learning and adaptation.

11.1 Dealing with Competition and Market Changes

Competition and market changes are inevitable in any business venture.

Here's how you can navigate these challenges:

Focus on your unique value proposition: Clearly define what sets your business apart from competitors. Identify your unique strengths, whether it's exceptional customer service, innovative products, or specialized expertise. Emphasize these qualities to differentiate yourself in the market.

Monitor the competitive landscape: Stay informed about your competitors' activities, strategies, and offerings. Regularly conduct market research to identify emerging trends and potential areas of disruption. This knowledge will help you stay proactive and adapt your business accordingly.

Cultivate customer loyalty: Build strong relationships with your customers by providing exceptional experiences and personalized service. Engage with your customers through social media, email newsletters, or loyalty programs. The more connected your customers feel to your brand, the less likely they are to be swayed by competitors.

Foster innovation and agility: Encourage a culture of innovation within your business. Continuously seek ways to improve your products, services, and operational processes. Be open to experimentation and adapt quickly to market changes.

Collaborate with partners: Consider forming strategic partnerships with complementary businesses. By collaborating with others, you can expand your reach, share resources, and leverage each other's strengths to overcome competition and adapt to market changes.

11.2 Managing Time and Avoiding Burnout

As an entrepreneur, time management and avoiding burnout are crucial for maintaining productivity and well-being. Here are some strategies to help you:

Prioritize tasks: Identify the most important and high-impact tasks that align with your business goals. Use prioritization frameworks such as the Eisenhower Matrix or the 80/20 rule to focus on activities that yield the greatest results.

Delegate and outsource: Recognize that you can't do everything on your own. Delegate tasks to your team members or outsource non-core activities. This frees up your time to focus on strategic decision-making and high-value tasks.

Set boundaries: Establish clear boundaries between work and personal life. Define specific work hours and allocate time for relaxation, hobbies, and time with loved ones. Avoid the temptation to constantly be "on" and make self-care a priority.

Practice effective time management techniques: Utilize time management techniques such as Pomodoro Technique, time blocking, or productivity apps to optimize your work schedule and improve focus and efficiency.

Take breaks and recharge: Schedule regular breaks throughout the day to rest and recharge. Stepping away from work can help reduce stress and increase productivity when you return. Consider incorporating exercise, meditation, or other stress-relieving practices into your routine.

Seek support: Reach out to mentors, peers, or business support networks for guidance and support. They can offer valuable insights, advice, and motivation during challenging times.

11.3 Embracing Continuous Learning and Adaptation

In the ever-evolving digital landscape, continuous learning and adaptation are essential for success. Here's how you can embrace these principles:

Stay informed: Keep up with industry trends, technological advancements, and changes in consumer behaviour. Subscribe to relevant industry publications, attend conferences or webinars, and engage in online communities to stay informed about the latest developments.

Pursue professional development: Invest in your own growth by pursuing professional development opportunities. This could involve taking courses, acquiring certifications, or participating in workshops or seminars. Continuously expanding your knowledge and skills will keep you ahead of the curve.

Foster a learning culture within your team: Encourage a culture of continuous learning among your employees. Provide opportunities for training and development, and encourage them to share their knowledge and insights. Embrace a growth mindset that values learning and adaptation.

Embrace feedback: Actively seek feedback from customers, employees, and mentors. Feedback provides valuable insights into areas for improvement and helps you adapt your strategies accordingly. Approach feedback with an open mind and view it as an opportunity for growth.

Experiment and iterate: Be willing to experiment with new ideas, products, or marketing strategies. Embrace a mindset of iteration and improvement based on feedback and data. Embracing a culture of experimentation allows you to adapt quickly to changing market dynamics.

Stay motivated through purpose: Connect with your underlying purpose and mission as an entrepreneur. Remind yourself of the impact you want to make and the goals you're working towards. Surround yourself with a supportive network and seek inspiration from success stories and role models.

Overcoming challenges and staying motivated as an entrepreneur requires resilience, adaptability, and a growth mindset. By effectively managing competition, prioritizing time and well-being, and embracing continuous learning, you can navigate the ever-changing digital landscape and achieve long-term success.

ABOUT THE AUTHOR

Meet Dr. Chris Egbu, a force to be reckoned with in the realm of productivity and business success. With a wealth of knowledge and experience, he has become a trusted advisor to countless individuals and organizations seeking to unlock their full potential.

As a fellow of the esteemed Centre for Public Service Productivity & Development, Dr. Egbu has dedicated his life to the pursuit of excellence. His multifaceted career as a productivity coach, author, public speaker, and productivity auditor has allowed him to make a profound impact on the lives of others.

With an unwavering passion for helping individuals thrive, Dr. Egbu has captivated audiences around the world, from top executives to aspiring entrepreneurs. His dynamic presentations delve into the realms of productivity, management strategies, performance excellence, entrepreneurial development, and leadership. Through his electrifying talks, he ignites a spark within his listeners, propelling them towards unparalleled growth and success.

But Dr. Egbu's impact extends far beyond the stage. As a Certified Management Consultant, he has personally guided countless individuals in transforming their dreams into reality.

Dr. Egbu's impressive track record speaks for itself. He has resuscitated struggling businesses, steering them away from the brink of bankruptcy and towards a path of prosperity. His strategic insights and innovative approaches have elevated countless organizations, empowering them to increase their net worth and thrive in the face of challenges.

Prepare to embark on a transformative journey guided by the expertise of Dr. Chris Egbu. Your quest for productivity, business acumen, and profound growth starts here.